Snap
books®

T0084550

TOP
BASKETBALL
TIPS

BY REBECCA RISSMAN

Consultant: Kristin Krusemark, Basketball Coach
Mankato Area Public Schools, Mankato, Minnesota

CAPSTONE PRESS
a capstone imprint

Snap Books are published by Capstone Press
1710 Roe Crest Drive, North Mankato, Minnesota 56003
www.mycapstone.com

Library of Congress Cataloging-in-Publication Data.
Names: Rissman, Rebecca, author
Title: Top basketball tips / by Rebecca Rissman.
Description: North Mankato, Minnesota : Capstone Press, a Capstone imprint,
    [2017] | Series: Snap books. Top sports tips | Audience: Age 8–14. |
    Audience: Grade 4 to 6. | Includes bibliographical references and index.
Identifiers: LCCN 2016026022| ISBN 978-1-5157-4719-2 (library binding) |
    ISBN 978-1-5157-4725-3 (pbk.) | ISBN 978-1-5157-4743-7 (eBook PDF)
Subjects: LCSH: Basketball—Juvenile literature.
Classification: LCC GV885.1 .R57 2017 | DDC 796.323--dc23
LC record available at https://lccn.loc.gov/2016026024

EDITORIAL CREDITS

Editor: Gena Chester
Designer: Veronica Scott
Media Researcher: Eric Gohl
Production Specialist: Kathy McColley

PHOTO CREDITS

Capstone Studio: Karon Dubke, 8–9 (bottom), 10, 11, 12 (right), 13, 14, 15, 29; iStockphoto: Matt Brown, 23 (left); Newscom: Icon SMI/Robin Alam, 25 (bottom), Icon Sportswire/Rich Graessle, 20 (front), TNS/Nuccio DiNuzzo, 6 (bottom), 28, ZUMA Press/Jon-Michael Sullivan, 27 (bottom), ZUMA Press/Kevin E. Schmidt, 22, 24, ZUMA Press/Manny Crisostomo, 26, ZUMA Press/Nicole Fruge, 4 (bottom), ZUMA Press/Taylor Jones, 19; Shutterstock: Aspen Photo, 7 (left), Jamie Roach, 18 (top), Jeff Schultes, 16, Julwitul Tongbai, cover (basketball), 1, 4 (top), 6 (top), 7 (right), 8 (top), 12 (left), 18 (bottom), 20 (back), 23 (right), 25 (top), 27 (top), 32, Opka, 5, Sergey Kuznecov (basketball court background), Tetiana Yurchenko, cover (hoop)

Printed in the United States of America.
052017   010554R

TABLE OF CONTENTS

Chapter 1

HOOP *Dreams*

History's first men's basketball game didn't look much like modern basketball. In fact the 1891 contest looked downright bizarre. It involved two nine-man teams, a soccer ball, and two peach baskets. In 1893 Smith College in Massachusetts modified the rules and organized the first women's basketball game. Those early players may not have known their game would lead to a major sport worldwide.

Today basketball is a popular, action-packed sport. It pits two five-player teams against each another as they race against the clock. Each team's goal is to score as many points as they can by shooting the ball into the opposing team's basket.

Know the Court

Basketball is played both indoors and outdoors on large, rectangular courts split into two halves. Two baskets are located at the opposite ends of the court. The basket is usually 10 feet (3 meters) high. Each basket is surrounded by the three-point shooting line, free throw line, and the free throw lane. Baselines and sidelines surround the court and determine what is out of bounds.

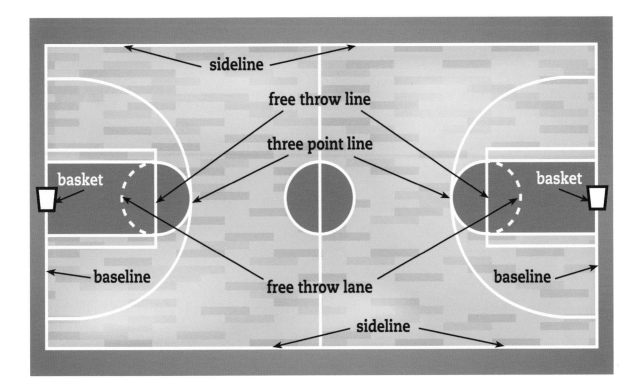

Basketball Basics

To move down the court, players can either pass the ball to a teammate, or they can **dribble** the ball. Once they get close enough to the basket, they can try to score. Players from the opposite team can try to prevent this by stealing the ball or blocking a shot.

Basketball is all about possession. The team that is in possession of the ball is the offense. The other team is the defense. The team on offense tries to score points. The team on defense tries to stop offense from getting points and to gain possession of the ball. The offense lose possession when the defense steals or blocks a shot, after they make or miss a basket, or after an illegal move, such as **traveling**. A foul is an illegal move that a player does to her opponent and can sometimes result in loss of possession. This possession obsession means that basketball games are fast and furious.

GET *Started*

Girls interested in joining a basketball team should explore their options. Some leagues are extremely competitive. Others focus mostly on making sure girls have fun. Ask an adult to help you find the right league for you. Your area may have leagues associated with your school or community.

dribble—to push the ball continuously into the ground with the fingertips

travel—to move both feet while holding the ball; to take three or more steps after dribbling the ball

Hit the Court

There are five different player positions on a basketball team. Each position is slightly different and plays an important role in both offensive and defensive play.

The point guard is often the leader of the team. She is a great passer, dribbler, and ball handler. She works to get the ball to other players near the basket. The shooting guard's main job is to get rebounds and take shots outside the free throw lane. The forward has many skills. She's an accurate shooter, a fast runner, and a great ball handler. The power forward uses her quick feet and sturdy body in the lane for shooting and rebounding. She's also great at defense. The center is usually the tallest player on the team. She's an accurate shooter close to the basket and is skilled at rebounding.

~ Tip ~

Work with your coach to decide which position is the best fit for you and your skills.

Chapter 2

SWEAT BEFORE *You Score*

Basketball is an incredibly challenging sport. Players spend almost an entire game sprinting, shooting, blocking, and chasing the ball up and down the court. They train by doing **cardiovascular** exercises, such as running, biking, or swimming, to build **endurance**. Basketball players also have to have quick reflexes and strong, flexible muscles. To prepare for the season, players often spend months working on their fitness.

Stretch First, Shoot Second

Incorporate these simple stretches into your pre-workout routine to ensure that your muscles are ready to work.

RECLINED LEG STRETCH

Lie on your back with both legs outstretched. Bend your right leg, interlace your fingers around your knee, and bring your leg to your chest. Use your hands to press your leg closer to your chest to get a deeper stretch. Switch sides.

SEATED TWIST

Sit with your legs crossed. Reach your right hand to your left knee or onto the floor, and bring your left hand behind your back. Look over your left shoulder and gently twist. Switch sides.

~ Tip ~

Hold each stretch for at least 10 seconds.

SHOULDER WALL STRETCH

Stand with your chest against a wall. Extend your right arm, palm facing up, out to your side so that it is level with your shoulder. Press your right pinkie and inner arm into the wall. Slowly begin to rotate your hips and feet to the left while keeping your right arm pressing into the wall. Stop when the stretch becomes intense. Switch sides.

---

cardiovascular—relating to the heart and blood vessels; cardiovascular exercises challenge the heart and lungs

endurance—the ability to keep doing an activity for long periods of time

Endurance on the Court

After you've stretched, you're ready to sweat it out with cardio. Cardio exercises will help take your endurance to the next level.

INVISIBLE JUMP ROPE

Pretend you are holding a jump rope and start jumping! Switch up your jump rope routine by jumping on one leg at a time. This exercise provides a good cardio workout and strengthens leg muscles at the same time.

Cardio only gets athletes so far. Basketball players need **agility** to move quickly in any direction.

CROSSOVERS

Run the length of the court facing sideways with your left foot leading. Cross your right foot over and behind as you progress down the court. Once you get to the end, face the same side of the court and run with your right foot leading the way.

LINE SPRINTS

Sprint from the baseline to the free throw line, midcourt line, the opposite free throw line, and the opposite baseline. Sprint back to the first baseline after you reach each destination. Make sure to reach down and touch the lines before changing directions.

---

agility—the ability to move in a quick and easy way

Strength Training

Strength training exercises work to build muscle strength. Basketball players use muscles all over their body. Leg muscles help players jump high and run fast. Shoulder muscles provide strength for shooting. And core muscles provide the base and balance for all of your shoulder and legs muscles. Try these activities to get super strong.

Squat Jumps

Stand with your feet shoulder distance apart. Squat deeply, keeping your weight in your heels. Then explode into the air by jumping as high as possible. Land softly back on your feet in your shoulder-width stance. Repeat several times.

Walk the Plank

Start in a plank position. Keep your back and core tight as you walk your hands to the right and leave your feet where they are. Try to walk your hands in a complete circle.

~ Tip ~

For an added challenge in your Walk the Plank activity, add a push-up after every "step" you take with your hands.

Scissor Kicks

Lie on your back with arms flat on the ground at your sides. Bring feet up and together about 1 foot (0.3 m) off the ground. Bring your right foot up about 6 inches (15 centimeters). While you're doing that, bring your left foot down about 6 inches (15 cm). Don't rush! The more controlled the movements are, the more of a workout you'll get. Repeat the motion 20 times.

SHOOT FOR
the Hoop!

As soon as a basketball player gains possession of the ball, she has one goal in mind: to get it down the court and score. One way to move the ball down the court is to dribble it. To dribble, players bounce the ball with one hand. The most important part of dribbling is practice. The more you practice, the easier it will be to dribble around defenders or down the court.

~ *Tip* ~

Don't stare at the ball! Instead, use your ears and **peripheral vision** to keep track of the ball as you dribble. This way, you'll be able to watch what else is happening in the game.

Dribbling Mechanics

Before you start practicing, there are a few dribbling basics to keep in mind. Stand with your feet shoulder-distance apart and your knees slightly bent. Put your weight onto the balls of your feet. Keep your head lifted as you use your fingertips to press the ball down toward the floor. As it bounces back up into your hand, press it back down with plenty of force. Once you're comfortable, try walking and running while dribbling.

DRIBBLING *Drills*

Players need to practice dribbling a lot before it becomes a natural skill. The Front V Dribble Drill is a great place to start. Using your right hand, dribble the ball so that the bounces make a wide "V" shape in front of you. You'll have to move your hand from right to left to keep this up. After you're comfortable with the right side, switch hands.

Once you've mastered that drill, move on to a drum roll. Bend your knees and alternate hands as you dribble the ball as low and fast as you can. If you're doing this right, it will start to sound like a drum roll!

peripheral vision—what can be seen out of the sides of the eyes while looking straight ahead

Pass It On!

Another way to move the ball down the court is to pass it. There are several different types of passes, including the bounce pass and chest pass. Basketball players need to be strong, quick, and accurate with their passes. Otherwise, they might miss their target or have their pass stolen by the other team.

Chest Pass Mechanics

Start by holding the ball close into your chest. Keep your elbows tucked into your sides. Keep your feet shoulder-distance apart and bend your knees slightly. Face the player who is receiving your pass. Take a strong step forward with one foot and push the ball straight at the player's chest with both hands. As you release the ball, let your palms flick outward.

Mechanics of a Bounce Pass

Begin as though you are going to throw a chest pass. Instead of aiming at your target's chest, aim to bounce the ball about two-thirds of the way there.

DANCE WITH
the Wall

Don't have a partner? Don't worry! Practice your passing solo with this drill. Start out standing about 6 feet (1.8 m) from a wall. Using your best form, throw a hard chest pass into the wall. When the ball bounces off, catch it. Chest pass into the wall again. Repeat 10 times. For added difficulty and endurance, chest pass against the wall while shuffling.

~ *Tip* ~

Try a bounce pass to move the ball around tall defenders.

Swish!

Layup! Jump Shot! Free throw! There are many types of shots in basketball, with values ranging from one to three points. Great basketball players get familiar with many different shots. Then they can be ready for anything that happens in a game. No matter what type of shot they're taking, basketball players have to use the right mechanics to be consistent, strong scorers.

Mechanics of a Jump Shot

Stand with your feet shoulder-distance apart and your knees slightly bent. Face the basket. Support the ball with your fingertips and keep your elbows tucked into your sides. Raise the ball so that it is shoulder height. Place your non-shooting hand on the side of the ball and bring your shooting hand to the back of the ball. Your non-shooting hand offers support, not power, in your shot. As you jump, press your shooting hand into the ball in a straight line toward the rim. Let your shooting wrist flick down as you release the ball.

PERFECT YOUR *Form*

Repetition is key to learning a new skill, especially in basketball. Try this drill to perfect your shooting mechanics even before you aim for the hoop.

Stand about 10 feet (3 m) away from your partner. Imagine that there is a hoop between the two of you. Use your very best form and shoot the ball. Your partner should be able to catch it without moving her feet. Alternate shooting with your partner over and over. The more you do this, the more comfortable you will be with your form.

When you've perfected the partner shoot with two hands, try it one handed. Use just your shooting hand to shoot the ball toward your partner. This will help you break the habit of using your non-dominant hand.

~ Tip ~

Your legs are powerful. Don't forget about them! Bend your knees and really spring up as you shoot longer distances.

layup—a shot made near the basket

jump shot—a shot made by jumping into the air and releasing the ball at the top of the jump

free throw—a shot made from behind a set line and without the threat of a defender; free throws are awarded because of a foul by an opponent

Mechanics of a Layup

Starting from the right side of the basket, dribble using your right hand as you jog toward the basket. When you're close to the basket, jump off your left foot and lift your right foot up into the air. As you jump, shoot with your right hand. Aim for the upper right corner of the box painted on the backboard. Switch all of these directions to the opposite side if you are approaching the basket from the left side.

~ Tip ~

Imagine a string is connecting your right elbow and knee. When you jump off your left foot, lift your right knee and elbow at the same time.

Free Throw Mechanics

The best part about a free throw? There's no defender! Set your body up the same way you would a jump shot. But don't jump! The shot won't count if you cross the free throw line before the ball hits the basket. Bend your knees into a squat. As you rise, raise your arms to take your shot. Shoot the ball from your fingertips, using the power from your legs to bring you onto your toes.

SNEAKY *Screens*

Sometimes an offensive player will want to free up a teammate from her defender for a pass, shot, or other move. A great way to do this is to use her body as a barrier in a **screen**.

Stand upright with your feet shoulder-distance apart. Square your chest to the defensive player you are screening, and cross your hands over your chest. Do not move!

screen—an offensive move in which the player holds still and uses her body to block an opponent

Chapter 4

DEFENSE!
Defense!

There are many parts to playing defense. One-on-one defense, zone defense, stealing, and rebounding are some key parts that every competitve player should know.

In one-on-one defense, one defensive player is assigned to one offensive player. She guards her opponent by mirroring all of her movements and attempting to take the ball from her. In zone defense, a defensive player is in charge of defending a particular area of the court. She guards any offensive player that comes into that part of the court.

Stand Like You Mean It

A good defensive stance goes a long way in stopping the offense. Square your hips and shoulders to the player you are defending. Bend your knees and have your feet shoulder-distance apart or a little bit wider. Extend both arms out to your sides with your palms facing forward. Stay between the player you are guarding and the basket by taking small, sliding steps from side to side.

Stealing

Defensive players can cause a **turnover** in the game by stealing the ball from the offense. When opponents are poor at dribbling and passing, steals come easily. But even the best offensive player can lose a ball to a defender.

Look for patterns in your opponent's offense. Does she always jab left and then break right? Does she dribble high across her body? Both present an opportunity for a steal. Stealing requires you to watch, wait, and anticipate.

~ Tip ~

In order for a steal to be legal, defensive players must not hit the offensive player's hands. If they do, it's considered a foul.

Rebounding

Players rebound when they catch a ball that didn't make it into the basket. Rebounding is a technique used by both the offense and defense. When an offensive player gets a rebound, she is trying to grab the ball and quickly try to make another shot or pass it to a teammate. When a defensive player gets a rebound, she is going to get the ball down the court so that her team can make a shot.

turnover—loss of possession of the ball

Mechanics of Rebounding

To get a rebound, get close to the basket. **Box out** the player you are guarding. This means you should try to get between the basket and the player, with your back to the player and your arms stretched out wide. As soon as the ball bounces off the rim, jump up to grab it. Pull it into your chest immediately with your elbows out to the sides. Pivot away from the basket and scan the court to decide on your next move.

~ *Tip* ~

After you've snagged a rebound, wait a second or so before you start dribbling it. This will reduce the chances that the other team will immediately steal it back.

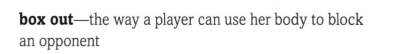

box out—the way a player can use her body to block an opponent

PUT IT ALL TOGETHER
with 3-2-1

The 3-2-1 drill puts all of your mechanics to the test. On a full court, have three offensive players take the ball up to their basket and try to score. Two other players are on defense. As soon as a player makes a basket, she runs to the other end of the court and goes on defense as the two defenders become offense and try to score against her.

Get the Point?

The most important part of basketball has little to do with who has the most points on the scoreboard. The point of the game is to have fun. Don't get too focused on who is winning or losing. Instead, try to be the best teammate you can be, and remember to always be a good sport.

GLOSSARY

agility (uh-GI-luh-tee)—activities that help athletes become better at moving quickly in different directions

box out (BOKS OUT)—a technique used to block you opponent from getting the rebound

cardiovascular exercise (kahr-dee-oh-VAS-kyoo-luhr EK-suhr-syz)—relating to the heart and blood vessels; cardiovascular exercises challenge the heart and lungs

dribble (DRI-buhl)—to push the ball continuously into the ground with the fingertips

endurance (en-DUR-enss)—the ability to keep doing an activity for long periods of time

peripheral vision (puh-RIF-ur-uhl VIZH-uhn)—what can be seen out of the sides of the eyes while looking straight ahead

pivot (PIV-uht)—to turn on one foot

possession (poh-seh-suhn)—having the ball

screen (SKREEN)—an offensive move in which a player holds still and uses her body to block an opponent

traveling (TRAV-uhl-ing)—moving while holding the ball

turnover (turn-OH-vur)—loss of possession of the ball

READ MORE

Doeden, Matt. *Fantasy Basketball Math: Using Stats to Score Big in Your League.* Fantasy Sports Math. North Mankato, Minn.: Capstone Press, 2017.

Forest, Christopher. *Side-by-Side Basketball Stars: Comparing Pro Basketball's Greatest Players.* Side-by-Side Sports. North Mankato, Minn.: Capstone Press, 2015.

Stuckey, Rachel. *Full Court Press: Basketball Skills and Drills.* Basketball Source. New York: Crabtree Publishing, 2016.

INTERNET SITES

FactHound offers a safe, fun way to find Internet sites related to this book. All of the sites on FactHound have been researched by our staff.

Here's all you do:
Visit *www.facthound.com*

Type in this code: **9781515747192**

Check out projects, games and lots more at
www.capstonekids.com

INDEX